Multisided Platforms:
Evaluating Launch Conditions

Robert Hughes

A publication in the Creating Business Angles Series.

Multisided Platforms: Evaluating launch conditions
by Robert Hughes

Published in 2021 by Hughes Books an imprint of Hughes Consulting Limited
NZ Business number 9429030579200
UK Registered number 05067369

www.HughesBooks.info

Alpha Edition
© Robert David Hughes 2021

This book is copyright. Apart from fair dealing for the purpose of private study, research, criticism or review, permitted under the Copyright Act 1994, no part may be reproduced by any process without the prior permission of the copyright holders and the publisher.

ISBN 978-0-473-61145-3 (Paperback)
ISBN 978-0-473-61146-0 (Epub)

A catalogue record of this book is available from the National Library of New Zealand Te Puna Matauranga o Aotearoa.

Contents

Introduction   1

Chapter 1
Positive cross-group feedback phenomenon   10

Chapter 2
Declining cost economies phenomenon   20

Chapter 3
Pricing and the launch of an MSP+   33

Chapter 4
Solving the challenges of launch and continued relevance   43

Chapter 5
Evaluating the potential of an emergent MSP+   49

Key influences on the work   55

Abbreviations   56

Glossary   57

List of figures

Figure 1
Examples of different MSP+s that enable groups of users to interact   2

Figure 2
Bar graph depicting the allocation of total value added to two user groups and the platform operator   6

Figure 3
The relationship between price, benefit and demand of a product   12

Figure 4
Significant disruption in the market, and a shift in the demand curve from an increased taste for the product from learning to use the product   13

Figure 5
Graphs depicting the relationship of demand by receivers for different levels of access to senders as demand curves and participation curve   14

Figure 6
Graph showing positive cross-group feedback activated where senders preference curve is above receivers preference curve within the addressable market   17

Figure 7
Graph illustrating the impact of a change in price on the senders participation curve   18

Figure 8
Activity type matrix showing the taxonomy of the 16 sentinel activity types   22

Figure 9
High level value network map for a universal (monopoly) postal service and its forerunner   30

Figure 10
Two-sided market pricing framework   37

Figure 11
Illustrative suite of variants of a product offering increasing perceived net benefits and value-for-money and the impact on increasing sales to senders due to an increase in number of users from the cross-group effect   42

Figure 12
Coat hanger model used as an analogy for the conditions for an MSP+   54

Introduction

Scope

This book deals with a specific type of organisation, the multisided platform (MSP) that operates in multisided markets with positive feedback effects (MSP⁺). These are some of the most exciting and valuable but rare organisations. Examples can be found in a variety of settings from postal delivery, shopping malls, print publishing, open-source software projects, through to internet based social media, to name a few instances. The challenges in establishing a business venture of this type are quite unlike those faced by other organisations that operate in a single-sided market or are platform businesses without cross-group effects. Be under no illusion, the likelihood of success in creating an MSP⁺ is small. The reason for this is that to launch, the MSP⁺s must overcome the obstacle of reaching critical mass. The platform's products must offer enough benefit for each of the multiple parties transacting over the platform for them to change their current behaviour and join the platform and then want to remain on the platform. If critical mass is achieved, then positive feedback effects begin to operate, and growth can be very rapid. If not, the organisation operates in a single-sided market, which has a quite different set of business strategies.

A method to identify multisided market opportunities and assess whether there are prospects of it being developed into a multisided platform with positive feedback effects is presented. Identifying whether there are at least different types of customer groups involved, each being offered their own product does not mean that it is a business opportunity, and certainly not one capable of gaining scale to take advantage of any positive feedback effects. Selling products to one party to reach another party under the guise of removing transaction cost is not operating an MSP.

Definition of a multisided platform

MSP⁺s can occur at any point in a value network for example linking different stages in the value network such as, suppliers and buyers, and peer to peer linking of members within a group. They can also involve more than two groups, for example, senders, receivers and delivery agents. The MSP⁺ provides the systems and processes for interchanges between these various parties but not actually taking part in the contractual relationship between the parties. They do this by removing shared transaction cost between the transacting parties. Having said this there are contractual and institutional arrangements covering their operations and relationships with each of the user groups which mean that they may be forced to take on some elements of the contractual relationship. The key features of MSP⁺s can be illustrated by the friction that various platforms remove to enable a party to interact with a counter party, some examples are shown in Figure 1.

Figure 1 *Examples of different MSP⁺s that enable groups of users to interact*

Friction removed	Platform	User groups
Letter and small parcel delivery	Universal postal network	Senders and receivers
Information discovery	Search engine	Seekers and suppliers of information/ advertisers
Supplier discovery	Directory with advertising	Buyers and merchants/ advertisers
Price discovery and exchange	Auction	Buyers and sellers
Supplier discovery	Advertising supported media	Potential buyers and advertisers
Candidate discovery	Introduction agent	Employers and job candidates
Shopping mall	Market place	Buyers and merchants

In each of these examples the MSP⁺ involves a platform consisting of production processes, and at least two parties (generically called senders and receivers to acknowledge the early MSP⁺, the universal postal network) who transact directly with one another through the facilities of the platform – that is it provides a way of intermediating in a value network. As an illustration, in the simplest case of trade in a marketplace, suppliers deal directly with buyers with no involvement from the intermediary providing the platform. Frequently, the relationship between suppliers and buyers is through an intermediary such as a reseller. Where this is the case the direct customer relationship with the buyer is held by the reseller and not the supplier. Like resellers, MSP[+] facilitate buyers acquiring products from suppliers, but unlike resellers they enable buyers to deal directly with suppliers.

Interactions on MSPs are associated with cross-group feedback effects. Cross-group feedback effects occur where actions by one group cause change in the behaviour of another group. They are different to the more commonly found within-group social network feedback effects, such as the word-of-mouth effect where users tell other users but cause no change in behaviour to another user group. Good examples of the word-of-mouth effect come from the film industry where some films rapidly gain a high degree of notoriety.

The examples given so far are of positive cross-group feedback effects, but this feedback also can be negative or neutral. A gift registry is an example of an MSP with no cross-group feedback effect. Negative feedback effects occur in media (print, radio and television) where there can be strong negative reaction to too much advertising. As might be expected with intergroup interactions there are no universal rules. While negative feedback effects occur widely in media, they are not universal. The notable exceptions to this rule are fashion trade directories with most of the pages taken up with advertisements. For fashion trade directories, the more high-quality high fashion advertisements there are in an issue the more attractive it is to more fashion-conscious readers.

Having said this, positive feedback effects can be associated with organisations that are not MSPs. Supermarkets and department stores are resellers and not an MSP because they control the relationship with buyers, and separately with suppliers. These organisations can exhibit positive feedback effects attracting more buyers to the store – in this case buyers are attracted by the range of complementary products. In turn, the greater this foot traffic, the more suppliers are attracted to want to have their products stocked by the store (this is a product-range feedback effect). It is important to note that while positive cross-group feedback effects are sometimes associated with organisations, their existence does not mean that the organisation is an MSP. The key feature is that an MSP facilitates transactions between at least two parties who transact directly with one another through the facilities of the platform. The platform does not insert itself in the value network to separate buyers from their suppliers (who indeed may be a reseller).

While this book deals with pure MSP$^+$s, that does not imply that organisations operating an MSP$^+$ may not have functioning alongside it one or more single-sided business models to exploit the platform and its cross-group effects. One of the purposes of this book is to show that the operation of an MSP$^+$ is so different to operating in a single-sided market that neglect of the fundamentals of the MSP$^+$ will prevent it from escaping working in a single-sided market. Operating an MSP$^+$ requires quite a different set of skills to those needed in a single-sided market. This book informs ways to: design and create new MSP$^+$s; maintain and increase the value of existing MSP$^+$s; and leverage existing MSP$^+$s into new business opportunities. In doing this it describes a framework for evaluating the potential for success in taking to market a perceived MSP$^+$ opportunity.

Allocation of value added to the parties to a platform

Ensuring that each user group gains enough benefit from joining and participating on the platform is dependent on several factors. A depiction of the allocation of value added created by a platform is shown in Figure 2. The platform operator, however, wants to do this in such a way as to increase the share of the value added they can capture – that is their profit. The determinants of the allocation of the value added created by the platform are:

- The perceived benefit of the platform's products to the user groups.
- This in turn is influenced by benefit derived by users from the cross-group effect, and any change in taste for the product.
- The price to make use of the platform including the cost for ancillaries.
- The transaction costs borne by users in making use of the platform, some of which may be one-off and may constitute a barrier to use.
- Affordability.
- The state of competition in the market.

For users of the platform, the net benefit received is its value-for-money, which is the perceived benefit derived from using the platform, less the price to use the platform less the transaction costs involved in acquiring and using/consuming the product. At its most simple level value is allocated to each user group based on maximising value-for-money (perceived benefit for the price), subject to budget constraints.

Figure 2 also shows the contribution of delivery agents to the creation of value added by the platform. In this example, the price paid to delivery agents is a cost to the platform, and delivery agents do not share in the value added created by the platform. In this sense, workers in the gig economy who accept low wages are creating more value added to be shared between the platform operator and the user groups. They do not get to share in the value added. An increase in the price to delivery agents is increased cost to operating the platform. Sourcing work as a delivery agent where the platform provider determines the remuneration, is quite different to an introduction platform that removes transaction costs of candidate discovery from employers and job candidates. An introduction platform does not insert itself in the employment relationship between the transacting parties who set their own price and conditions of employment.

Figure 2 *Bar graph depicting the allocation of total value added to two user groups and the platform operator*

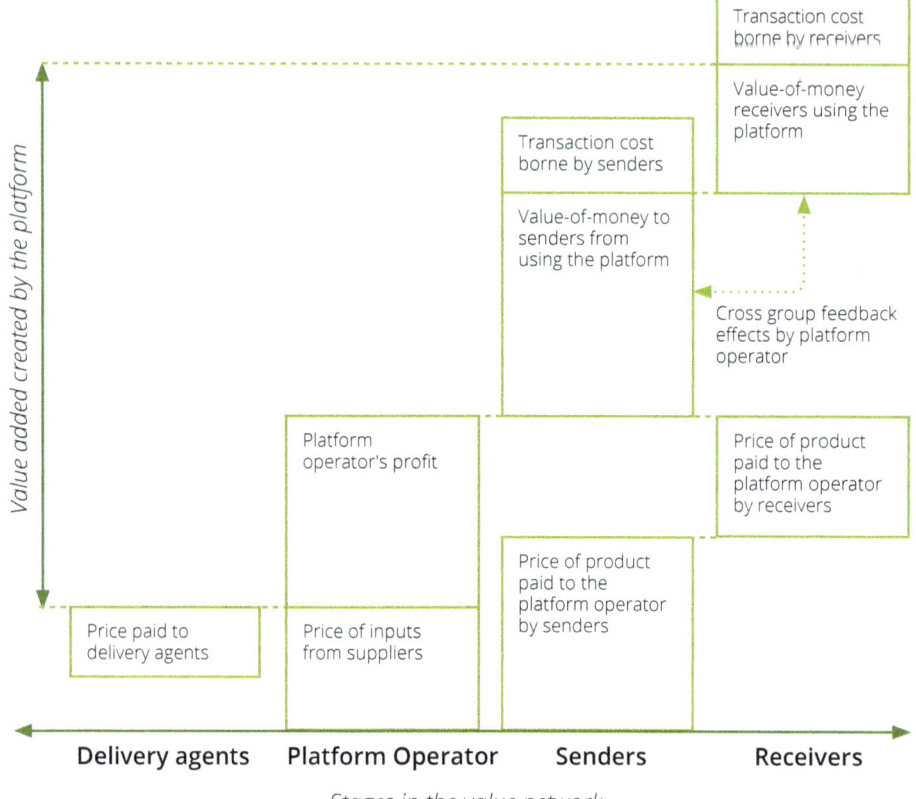

Value of the MSP⁺

A business angle encapsulates the perceived business opportunity commercialised through products, and the way that it is to be realised through an activity type that is embodied in a production process. Production processes have organisational structure, activity type that use production technology with appropriate knowhow, systems and processes, resources, and contractual obligations to transform inputs into deliverable outputs.

With an estimate of the planned sales volume, the value of the share of value added captured by the platform operator can be calculated. An established method for valuing business ventures is the Free Cash Flow (FCF) method. This method calculates the net present value of expected income for the expected expenditure made, over its expected lifetime. Present value is the value today of a future amount taking into consideration the time value of money – i.e. the discount rate. Adding the present values of all expected cash inflows and outflows for all periods over a venture's expected lifespan gives the net present value. For example, suppose $1,000 is invested to receive $300 net profit at the end of each year, for five-years. With a 10 percent a year discount rate and using the compound interest rate formula, the present value of the free cash flows are: the initial outlay of -$1,000; $273 (i.e. $300 ÷ 1.1^1) net profit received at the end of the first year; $248 (i.e. $300 ÷ 1.1^2) received at the end of the second year; $225 (i.e. $300 ÷ 1.1^3) at the end of year three; $205 (i.e. $300 ÷ 1.1^4) for year four; and finally $186 (i.e. $300 ÷ 1.1^5). Adding these discounted net cash flows together gives the Net Present Value, a total of $137. That is the initial investment (of $1,000) plus a surplus of $137 and it is the FCF value (business value or simply value) and is the price that would be expected to be paid for the investment.

Expected net profit is the residual expected cash income after cash outflows. Income, in the simple example above, is the revenue from the users. Sometimes use of the MSP⁺ is free to one of more user groups with revenue from applications products. Cash outflows cover: operational cost to operate the platform, cost of stimulating positive cross-group feedback, and costs for acquiring and maintaining systems and processes.

There is uncertainty in the expected cashflows because the actual amount may turn out to be different to that planned. There is uncertainty because: future prices are unknown; miscalculations of the market opportunity; organisation ability and other arrangements put in place turn out to operate differently from what was planned, for example. Uncertainty is usually referred to as risk, although risk is a particular type of uncertainty. Expected income and expenditure includes that from speculation and ability to manage uncertainty. Uncertainty adds cost as the organisation endeavours to ensure its business plans are met and to ensure that the organisation is resilient to unexpected events. On the other hand, uncertainty can bring lucky breaks from identifying opportunities from which the organisation can benefit. The cost of uncertainty is commonly incorporated into the discount rate, increasing it. Increases in net profit and reductions in uncertainty increases the value of the organisation.

For the platform operator, the key components of the MSP⁺ profit equation, are:

Profit =   Revenue from transactions by senders and receivers;

less Investment and operational cost to operate the platform delivering services to the user groups;

less Cost of stimulating positive cross-group feedback;

less Cost to continually improve the value-for-money of the product to the user groups;

less Cost of uncertainty including the cost to gain critical mass.

MSP+ business angles rest on activating two economic phenomena

Implicit in the profit equation is the importance of scale to the success of an MSP⁺. Positive feedback between user groups grows sales, and some markets are large. Some production processes, such as software development, exhibit strong declining cost economies. An MSP⁺ business angle, therefore, can exploit two economic phenomena, one on each face of the business angle:

- positive cross-group effects; and
- declining cost economies.

Those organisations that succeed in activating these two economic phenomena can be large and profitable. In this context, to solve the profit equation requires:

- Finding a place in a value network for a product to facilitate transactions between multiple parties without taking part in the transaction.
- Designing a product (including its supporting production process and contract) that removes significant shared transaction costs.
- Implementing a production process that realises sufficient declining cost economies for the organisation to be valuable.
- Addressing the product launch considerations to achieve critical mass.
- Stimulating and maintaining strong positive cross-group feedback between the user groups once critical mass is achieved.

Each of these matters is discussed in this book. The structure followed in the remainder of this book is first to explain the positive cross-group effect, and the declining cost economies phenomena. A framework to model the role of price in the launch of an MSP$^+$ is then described. The framework is applied to the launch challenge faced in establishing a new MSP$^+$. The final chapter presents a discussion on the identification and evaluation of the prospects to successfully launch an MSP$^+$.

Chapter 1
Positive cross-group feedback phenomenon

Demand relationship

This chapter explains the determinants of usage of a platform. Put simply, total sales of a product are determined by its price, subject to the buyers' budget, and several other determinants. The conceptual relationship between price and the resultant sales is described in the aggregate demand curve. An example of this curve is depicted in the left-hand diagram in Figure 3. The downward slope of the curve is typical of a normal product, and is measured by the price elasticity of demand which is calculated as the proportionate change in quantity that results from a small proportionate change in price, keeping all other factors constant – this caveat is important because there are a range of other relevant determinants of demand.

Each product has a set of perceived benefits. Where a product has substitutes, sales of the substitute impact sales of the product. This relationship is measured as the cross-product elasticity of demand. Perfect substitutes have a cross-product elasticity of demand of positive one. This means that products with different perceived benefits can be compared on a value proposition map. Figure 3 shows, in the right-hand diagram, three products offering different perceived benefits, which are priced to provide constant value-for-money. The left-hand diagram shows their corresponding demand curves with, in this representation of total sales, the demand curve shifting to the right with increased perceived benefit.

As set out in Figure 2, for a buyer there are three components to value-for-money: the perceived benefit, less the price of the product less the transaction costs involved in acquiring and using/consuming the product, the occurrence of which may be at different points in time. An important way MSP⁺s improve value-for-money is by removing shared transaction costs, and this is achieved through product, contract, and process design. Even where a product is free, there may be competing products that provide better value-for-money because of low transaction costs, and therefore preferred by buyers. In the following discussion price includes the additional costs incurred by the buyer in consuming/using the products provided by the platform. For example, in sending a letter through the postal network the price is the cost of the stamp, the envelope and of creating the content – this is referred to as full price. The other elements of the cost of using/consuming a product reduce its benefit. In calculating cost the total of all elements of cost users face in transacting with one another must be included, be they the price of using the platform, ancillary costs to do that, as well as the transaction costs associated with finding and using the platform. These costs are offset against the perceived benefit derived from using the platform, and the residual is the value-for-money. The value-for-money must be positive but is different for each user group.

Other determinants that cause the demand curve to shift are: change in income of buyers, change in taste for the product, and various feedback effects such as social network, cross-product, and cross-group effects. The elasticity of demand can also change with change in social, technological, and institutional conditions. These changes can be significant. For example, in the days of international toll calls the price elasticity of demand was in the order of -3 (meaning that demand was elastic and very sensitive to change in price, and at a high price usage was limited), whereas internet based calling has an implied price elasticity of greater than -0.3 (meaning that price is inelastic and has little impact on demand and at a low price its use is ubiquitous).

Figure 3 *The relationship between price, benefit and demand of a product*

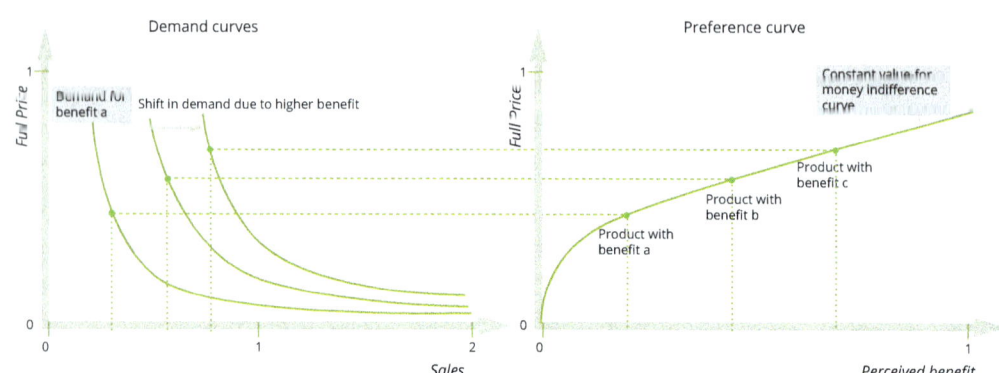

Note to figure: Elasticity of demand for: price of -0.5, taste of 1, and preference of -0.5. Perceived benefits of the products are 0.25, 0.5, and 0.75.

Market disruption

Market disruption is a buyer experience that occurs when comparative value-for-money changes rapidly and significantly enough to be noteworthy, forcing a re-evaluation of buyers spending patterns. To illustrate this, Figure 4 shows the introduction of a new high value-for-money product. Products offering higher value-for-money are placed to the right and below the legacy value-for-money preference curve. Where the increase in value-for-money is from a reduction in price, as in Figure 4, then sales for the product increase from Q1 to Q2.

Where this disruption is significant, then usage from learning how to make more use of the product increases the taste for the product, increasing demand, and sales increase from Q2 to Q3 because of the demand curve shifting to the right. A significant disruption in the market, and a shift in the demand curve from an increased taste for the product can be accompanied by a change in the price elasticity of demand. The result is a new market with quite different characteristics from the initial market. For example, for personal and business communications, the email market is quite different to the antecedent postal mail market.

Figure 4 *Significant disruption in the market, and a shift in the demand curve from an increased taste for the product from learning to use the product*

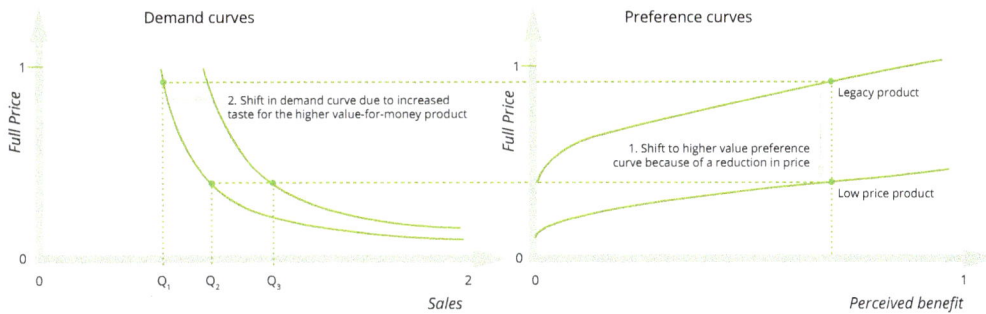

Note to figure: Elasticity of demand for: price of -0.5, taste of 0.5 and 1.0, and preference of -0.5; perceived benefit of 0.75 units, and price of $0.5 and 1.0 per unit.

Price and cross-group effects

A platform able to reach more receivers is of more use to senders, shifting the senders demand curve to the right, as shown in the bottom diagram in Figure 5. Similarly, receivers able to access more content shifts the receivers demand curve to the right. This occurred with the universal postal service, in making the receipt of mail free, people would accept letters. Prior to this, receivers were expected to pay to receive letters, this created a barrier (high shared transaction cost), and senders were unable to reliably get their correspondence in the hands of receivers. The relationship between the number of receivers reached, and transactions by senders over a platform, keeping price constant, is given in the senders participation curve in the top graph in Figure 5.

Figure 5 *Graphs depicting the relationship of demand by receivers for different levels of access to senders as demand curves and participation curve*

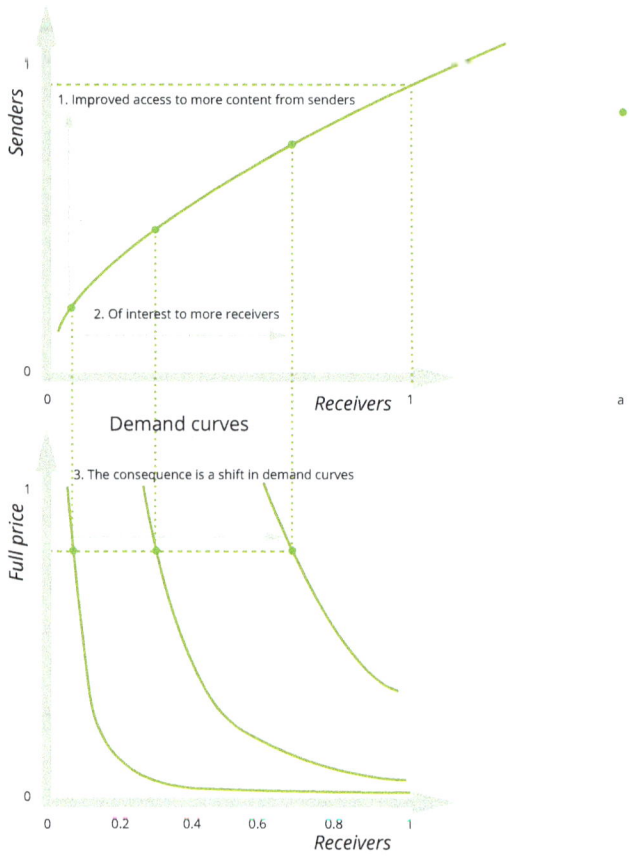

Note to figure: Parameter values are elasticity of demand for: price of -0.5, and cross-group of 2.

Cross-group relationships in a multisided market

In a two-sided market, demand and participation curves can similarly be developed to show the relationship between demand by receivers for content from senders. To explain how cross-group interactions operate in a two-sided market, the participation curves for the two user groups can be depicted in a single graph. The key to depicting the participation curves for senders and receivers in one graph is to express the two relationships in common variables, and this is achieved by equating content to the number of senders, and delivery reach to the number of receivers. Figure 6 is a graph with sender and receiver participation curves. The receivers participation curve shows that for access to the content of half the senders, all receivers will join the platform. Senders are not quite as enthusiastic. Two senders participation curves are shown, that for a lower and higher senders participation on a platform to reach receivers.

The intersections of the receivers and senders participation curves is the critical mass point. The critical mass point for the higher sender participation curve requires fewer users than that for the lower senders participation curve. Strength of the attraction to interact with the other user groups on a platform is an important factor in reducing the launch challenge to reach the critical mass point.

This representation of intergroup interaction in a two-sided market is useful in analysing some of the critical features of MSPs because it shows how changes on one side of the market impact the other side of the market. The arrows on the diagrams in Figure 6 show the compound direction of these

feedback effects. For example, in Figure 6, if the starting point were S number of senders on the platform, then R number of receivers are attracted to the platform. With R number of receivers for the higher participation curve, more senders (indicated by the upward arrow) are attracted to join the platform, this in turn attracts more receivers.

In this case, where the value proposition to both sides of the market is sufficiently strong to cause an overlap in the two curves (with senders participation curve to the right and above the receivers participation curve), then positive feedback effects operate to propel, in the absence of competitors and appropriate pricing, the demand to the maximum participation point. This feedback can be strong and the journey very rapid as demonstrated by growth of some internet businesses. MSP⁺s are valuable because of the market size which these feedback effects can open. However, even with strong cross-group effects, achieving critical mass can be an insurmountable hurdle.

To illustrate this, with S number of senders on the platform and a lower sender preference function, R number of receivers are insufficient to cause senders to remain on the platform, and the number of senders reduces (indicated by the downward pointing arrow in Figure 6). In this situation, feedback effects cause participation to collapse to the origin (bottom left-hand corner) - this is a single-sided market. This situation occurs where one or both value propositions are weak (the two curves do not intersect in the available addressable market) or, where they do, critical mass is not achieved. The vast majority of prospective MSP⁺s fail because of these two factors.

An organisation operating in a single-sided market would sell a product to one of the user groups, and market share is determined by product benefit, price, competition, availability, and notoriety. Organisations can spend significant sums on marketing to build notoriety to maintain and increase market share. This is because organisations operating in a single-sided market gain none of the advantages of positive cross-group feedback effects. That being said, other behavioural feedback effects can be used to promote notoriety, such as by word-of-mouth.

Figure 6 *Graph showing positive cross-group feedback activated where senders preference curve is above receivers preference curve within the addressable market*

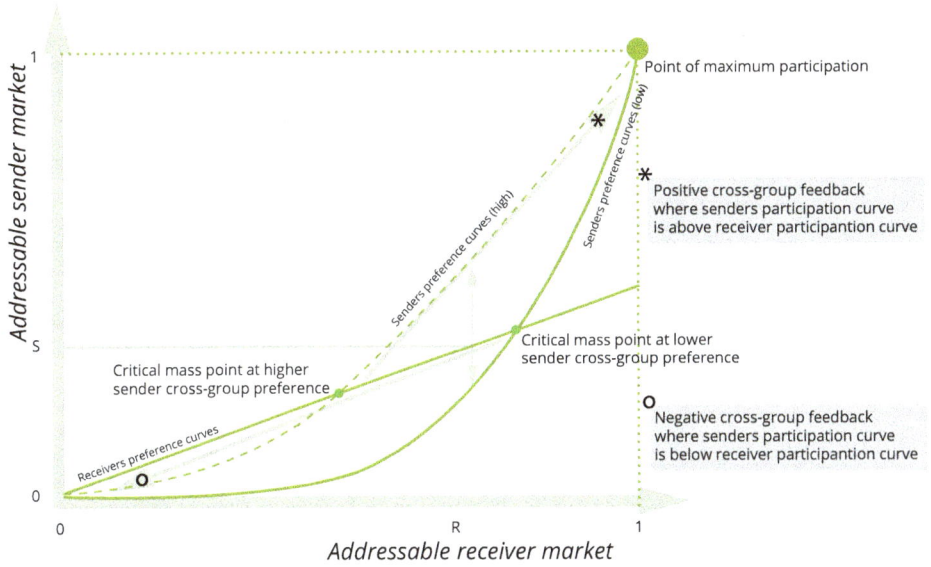

Note to figure: For receivers elasticities of demand for: price of -1, and cross-group of 1, and price to receivers of $0.5 per unit. Senders elasticities of demand for: price of -1, and cross-group of 2 (high) and 5 (low), and price to senders of $1 per unit.

Pricing impacts in multisided markets

Differences in benefits to the various parties to an MSP is most easily seen where there are strong positive cross-group feedback effects. Figure 7 shows the preference curves for senders and receivers at two different prices to senders. At the higher price shown in the diagram, the point of maximum participation attracts content from fewer senders than available in the addressable market. In addition, significant shares of the sender and receiver markets must be signed up to use the platform to reach the critical mass point. This increases the difficulty of the launch challenge, and therefore lowers the prospects of success.

This situation is contrasted with the position where the price to senders is lower. Two things are noteworthy about this position: first, the critical mass point is closer to the origin, meaning that fewer senders and receivers must be recruited to the platform for positive feedback effects to begin to operate. Second, the point of maximum participation encompasses the whole addressable market. There are two implications of this discussion:

High value propositions must be offered to both parties with the aim of stimulating high cross-group effects.

Different value is extracted from each group because of the strength of the cross-group feedback effects and price elasticity of demand. Pricing is therefore an important tool in addressing the launch challenge to reach critical mass.

Figure 7 *Graph illustrating the impact of a change in price on the senders participation curve*

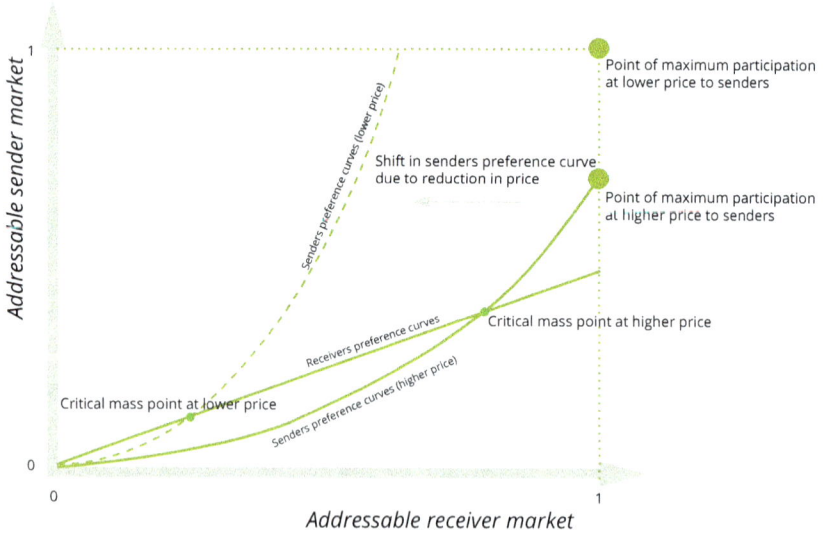

Note to figure: For receivers elasticities of demand for: price of -1, and cross-group of 1, and price to receivers of $0.5 per unit. Senders elasticities of demand for: price of -1, and cross-group of 2, and price to senders of $0.5 and 1.5 per unit.

Market size and planned sales

The positive cross-group effects operating on an MSP⁺s can unlock large markets. For existing MSP⁺s planned sales volumes can be estimated using econometric techniques from performance in existing markets. For opportunities involving new markets there may be no way to a priori deduce market size other than by launching a minimum viable product into the market. Before commencing market testing, some lessons are:

- Be clear what information you want to gain, and design a minimum viable product to demonstrate the product proposition to potential users to get that information.
- Prioritise gaining information over building solutions. It is easy to spend money on building solutions that have no market.
- Be aware that information gained from market testing is valuable. Intellectual property can be easily stolen without adequate safeguards.
- Set clear criteria on when to terminate the experiment.
- Learn from the information gained and use it to refine the business angle and launch strategy.

Stimulating cross-group effects is imperative

Sales are determined by several variables, such as: price, budget, income, perceived benefit, availability of substitutes and complements, and various feedback effects. The activation, and enhancement of positive cross-group feedback effects is a key feature of an MSP⁺ because it can rapidly increase market share.

Chapter 2
Declining cost economies phenomenon

Sources of declining cost economies

A feature of MSP⁺s is that once critical mass is achieved, they can be subject to rapid growth in users. MSP⁺s, therefore, are well placed to take advantage of declining cost economies. In addition, to drive uptake can require low prices (and much lower than the alternatives), and this requires production processes that deliver products at low average unit cost, and capable of generating high business value. A production process is the collection of capabilities and supporting information used by an organisation. A production process has organisational structure, activity type that uses production technology with appropriate knowhow, systems and processes, resources, and contractual obligations to transform inputs into delivered outputs.

For an organisation operating in a single-sided market, a business angle is the pairing of an activity type to the perceived opportunity to realise the aims within the constraints of the organisation. For an MSP, the business angle comprises a delivery method for each product set to each user group, and an acquisition method. A method requires knowhow, systems, processes and procedures to meet the specific requirements of the business angle. Four generic methods are used for acquiring inputs and four for delivering outputs. The assemble method is concerned with supplying products that are distinguishable from its component parts, the assign method with outsourcing for capacity, the aggregate method with providing access to a network or aggregation that benefits from the law of large numbers, and arbitrage with exploiting imperfections in the market. The taxonomy of activity types is given in the activity type matrix shown in Figure 8.

While a common delivery method is used by each product, each employs different production processes. There are 16 sentinel activity types classified based on a single delivery method and a single acquisition method. An MSP uses two generic activity types, related by a common acquisition method. There is, therefore, a set of 96 potential platform activity types to choose from to design an MSP business angle. Usually, as in the example of the postal operator (depicted in Figure 9) where the dominant platform activity type is Aggregate/Aggregate-Assemble (c. Network operator), a common delivery method is used for both user groups, so the effective range is the 16 sentinel activity types, but this need not be the case.

Realising low average unit cost from declining cost economies is important to the success of an MSP$^+$. Underpinning the assemble method are economies of scale and scope to drive the reduction in average unit cost. Declining cost economies of scale occur, for example, from high set-up costs (such as those faced by software developers in developing systems) in which average unit cost falls exponentially with number of uses. Declining cost economies in the assign method are due to improving coordination by ensuring close alignment of the interests between buyer and supplier where contracting for a capability is more efficient than internal supply. The aggregate method utilises declining cost economies from scale free networks and the law of large numbers. The existence of price differences, which arise from asymmetries in access to information, and high order costs is exploited by the arbitrage method to achieve declining cost economies. The takeout from this is that there are potentially a wide range of business angles that could create an MSP$^+$. Having said this, all the examples given in Figure 1 could use the Aggregate-Assemble activity type.

Figure 8 *Activity type matrix showing the taxonomy of the 16 sentinel activity types*

Guide to symbols:	⊕ Assembly	✥ Assign	✥ Aggregate	▪●▲✘ Arbitrage

| Method of acquiring inputs | Method of delivering outputs | | | |
	⊕	✥	✥	▪●▲✘
⊕	**a. Producer** Production of products by using inputs that require significant processing	**b. Outsource supplier** Supply of capacity based on utilising inputs that require significant pre-processing	**c. Network operator** Construction of a portfolio of purchasers of products that utilise inputs requiring significant transformation	**d. Developer** Resale of products derived from inputs requiring significant preparation
✥	**e. Systems integrator** Production of products utilising contracted operational capacity from third parties	**f. Lead contractor** Supply of capacity by utilising contracted operational capacity from third parties	**g. Consolidator** Construction of a portfolio of purchasers of products supplied from operational capacity contracted from third parties	**h. Agent** Resale of contracted operational capacity from third parties
✥	**i. Supplier cooperative** Production of products by engaging with a portfolio of input suppliers	**j. Underwriter** Supply of capacity by using capacity syndicated to several suppliers	**k. Insurer** Construction of a portfolio of purchasers of products that is syndicated to a portfolio of suppliers	**l. Auctioneer** Resale of products acquired from a range of input suppliers
	**m. Assembler** Production of products based on bought in sub-assembly componentry	**n. Broker** Supply of capacity by on-selling capacity from suppliers	**o. Aggregator** Construction of a portfolio of purchasers for products acquired for reselling	**p. Trader** Trading in products

Fortifying declining cost economies

One of the outstanding features of an MSP⁺ is that it can potentially realise more sources of declining cost economies, and the magnitude of those economies to a greater degree than an organisation operating in a single-sided market. This is because each method can contribute declining cost economies, and because the acquisition method and possibly also the delivery method carry additional volume as they service multiple user groups.

MSP⁺s that deliver products at lower average unit cost than competitors have developed core competencies in their production processes. Core competencies are a scarce resource, and have the unusual property that as their value increases, the value of the organisation increases. This is unlike other assets, whose value is determined only by demand and supply considerations. The consequences of this behaviour of core competencies are that they are: valuable; rare; difficult to imitate; and there is the organisational ability to exploit them, whether through accumulated experience, or operation of organisation wide systems and processes. Rarity and the ability to imitate the core competencies places them in the market, and the actions competitors could take to diminish the value of this scarce resource, and conversely actions by management to increase their value. Organisational ability gets to the heart of the adeptness to create core competencies, maintain them, and then leverage them into new business angles.

Additionally, production processes can be designed as hybrid activity types to exploit several different declining cost economies and in this way create complex business models. There are several reasons complex business models have been developed in conjunction with MSP⁺s. The first is the volume of transactions on a large MSP⁺ can also generate significant economies of size, for example investment in computer servers. The second reason is that the volume of transactions on large MSP⁺s generate data on customer behaviours, which in some cases can be used to hone products, and create new products to add new user groups to the platform, such as advertisers. MSP⁺s able to realise strong declining cost economies that create core competencies can parlay these into new business angles, such as computer server outsourcing products.

Product specification

Products are defined by their role in the value network. Product attributes include technical and functional specifications, availability in time and place, tangible and intangible experience qualities, sales service and after sales service and ceremony features. Products also have attributes of product meaning derived from the social, cultural and institutional setting. An important way that value-for-money can be improved is by reducing the transaction cost faced by users of the product. This is achieved through product and process design.

There are three types of products:

- Exchange products provide a high degree of readiness for use (through for example, custom and standardisation of specification) and transfer decision-making rights to consume or use, if not entirely, then at least for a period.
- Interface products are associated with the interaction between systems and processes, or channels for delivering finished products. Frequently, interface products reduce transaction costs and increase access. Interface products are sometimes bundled with an exchange product and may not be offered as a stand-alone product.
- Applications products extend the use of the provider's knowhow, systems and processes to new adjacent workflow processes or value networks by providing extra functionality. In addition to the application specific functionality, application products frequently utilise at least one exchange product (which can incorporate at least one interface product).

In its simplest form an MSP⁺ supplies an exchange and an interface product. In the case of the universal postal service, these two products are commonly bundled together in the form of a letter or parcel of prescribed weight and dimensions with authorised stamp lodged into a designated post box. Because the transaction costs that were removed by the universal postal service were so substantial, the limitations from standardisation (which enabled realising declining cost economies) were ameliorated by a range of different applications products that arose to increase the benefit to users of the postal MSP[+]. Examples of some application products provided by universal postal service providers are direct marketing mailing lists, printing of letters provided as electronic data files by the sender, and PO Boxes.

Market coordination mechanisms are the contractual relationships between the two transacting parties. Buyers use a range of different contractual relationships when working with suppliers. The most appropriate arrangement provides the most economical purchase of inputs to support a highly productive production process. The considerations influencing the choice of the preferred contractual relationship are whether:

- The product can be clearly defined and specified at the outset.
- Prospective suppliers are prepared to make the investment required to deliver the product.
- The risk adjusted cost of failure by the provider to the buyer is high.
- Poor performance by the supplier is easily identifiable and can be monitored, and the cost of mitigating that risk is low.

Where these considerations are simple to address then market exchanges and simple contracts are most efficient, and where they are not, a range of different types of contractual arrangements have been developed. These contracts involve more transaction cost. The use of 'complex' contractual types is an indicator of high transaction cost. Product and process design plays an important role in simplifying the contract used. Therefore, a way that platforms can reduce transaction costs is to simplify the contract type used for the product, and this is achieved by simplifying and standardising the product specification and the service delivery process.

Product and process design to remove friction

The friction faced in transacting are:

- search costs – all costs associated with locating a party including the cost of making a second-best choice because the first best party could not be located (e.g. in buyers trying to locate suppliers); and
- shared/duplicated transaction costs between the transacting parties. Transaction costs are all costs incurred from the time of the desire to commence a transaction through to its satisfactory conclusion (e.g. credit cards make it easier for buyers to buy and sellers to get paid).

How this process operates can be illustrated with an example from venture capital finance:

The funding process involves would-be-entrepreneurs presenting their case for funding to perspective backers. A significant hurdle faced by new entrepreneurs is to find investors who would consider their proposal. Compounding the search costs, new entrepreneurs can waste resources and their personal enthusiasm contacting established institutions like trading banks - who do not have products for this type of financing. The existence of two distinct groups (entrepreneurs and investors), and high search costs provides an opportunity for the creation of an MSP which facilitates new entrepreneurs locate and pitch to potential equity investors. The platform takes no part in the relationship established between the two groups instead it earns a fee on funds raised through access to the platform. Having established a relationship with investors another high search cost they face, should they want to sell these shares, is finding buyers for shares in unlisted companies. An extension could be to provide a secondary market by listing shares for sale in private unlisted companies.

This idea removes search costs for two groups (1) early stage entrepreneurs and investors; and (2) buyers and sellers of shares in private unlisted companies. However, this idea offers nothing to reduce shared/duplicated transaction costs of the parties – costs such as the veracity of the information being provided.

The pain points can be identified by mapping the customer journey to buy and use a product. Having identified an opportunity to remove friction, this immediately raises questions about the source of the friction, its significance, and what can be done about it? The point of departure for identifying and refining an MSP⁺ opportunity is to locate groups of users who transact with one another. Then, having established this, to identify:

- The other parties with whom they transact frequently and could also benefit from reductions in search and transaction costs. For example, through expanded access to existing products and users or through reduced cost to launch new products.
- New opportunities to reduce shared transaction and search costs between these parties.
- The introduction of new parties able to reduce transaction costs, and thereby reforming the shape of the value network.

While all MSPs must deliver transaction and/or search cost savings, this is not the whole story. The design of products with high product meaning is also important. Product meaning refers to how consumers relate to a product because of connotations associated with its physical, functional, symbolic and cultural attributes. In saying this, it is insufficient to offer products with high product meaning without improvements in value-for-money to both parties, usually in the form of cost savings or brand association. High product meaning is especially important where there are competing offerings in the market.

Reforming the value network by designing out friction

To reiterate, an MSP⁺ inserts itself into an existing value network to enable the parties to transact directly with one another and in doing so redraws the value network, creating a new different value network. Transacting over the platform removes friction between the two transacting parties. This is one of the distinguishing features of an MSP⁺, and is a reason for users to use it. This experience must provide better value-for-money than that achievable through alternatives.

As an example, Figure 9 shows the high-level value network for a universal (monopoly) postal service removing the shared transaction cost of senders and receivers contacting one another by letter or small parcel. The value network map shows the key participants and stages in the value network and the relative market share of customers (placed on the right-hand side of the map), and providers and in turn their suppliers (placed on the left-hand side). The map shows the market share of each group of participants. Of interest is what happens at the boundary between stages in the value network and this is where shared search and transaction costs occur, specifically:

- The use of interface, exchange and application products that can be provided by the platform.
- Market coordination mechanisms to use the platform.
- Market size.

In some instances where an MSP⁺ becomes widely adopted, legislation may be necessary to protect users from monopolistic exploitation, or to provide users with rights that improve the benefit of using the platform.

The consequence of removing significant transaction costs is that the value network is reformed. In this regard, the process engineering methods to identify opportunities to remove transaction costs are quite different from those used in information management business analysis, and customer experience design, which are frequently constrained to improving current processes within a largely unchanged value network.

It may be difficult to identify the shared transaction costs because many workarounds may have been developed by the market to solve elements of those costs to each user group. In removing friction, the buyer need for these solutions disappears. In this sense, the existence and size of these workarounds is a gauge of the magnitude of the size of the transaction cost faced by transacting parties. The existence of additional products that make use of a platform, points to deficiencies in the products provided by the platform, and the existence of shared transaction costs. In this sense the existence of a large eco-system surrounding a platform could sow the seeds of its replacement through disruption. Identifying the eco-system is one of the purposes of compiling a value network map.

Extrapolating from this, new MSP$^+$s will themselves create new opportunities for workaround solutions and applications products. Even though a disrupting MSP$^+$ may remove substantial friction they can create an ecosystem for new products. These new products are frequently applications products. Figure 9 shows four applications products: for receivers: post box services and mailroom services; and for senders: mail house services and direct marketing services. Many different organisations may participate in the ecosystem. The creation of an ecosystem is an important way that platforms can improve the benefit to users from joining the platform.

Figure 9 *High level value network map for a universal (monopoly) postal service and its forerunner*

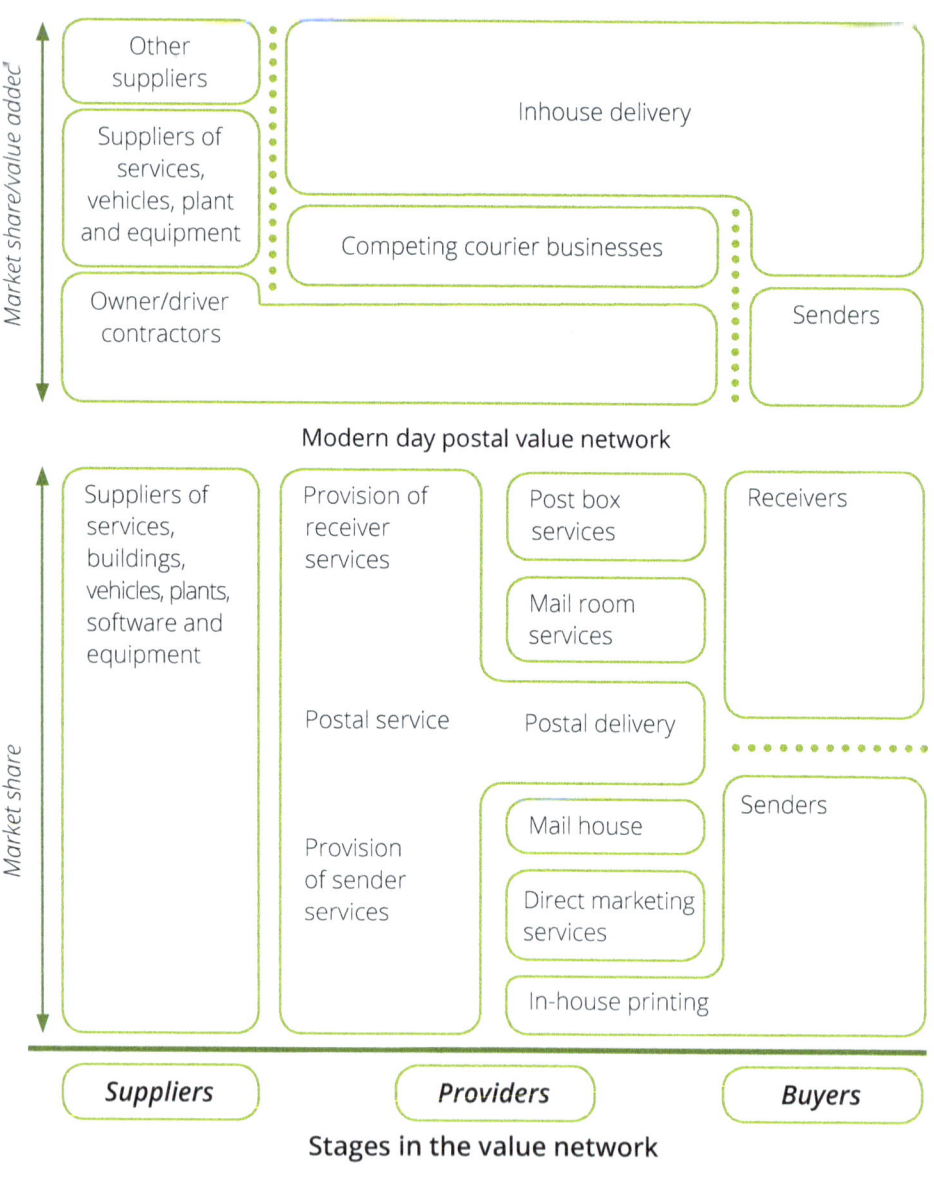

The value network map does not show that the size of the market created by the postal MSP⁺ is multiple times larger than the forerunner delivery service. Where there is a significant improvement in value-for-money, and low barriers to entry, then entry into the market could disrupt the market and gain first mover advantage. Unless the new disrupting offer is associated with increasing barriers to entry (such as from strong declining cost economies) others could soon follow. Where there are high barriers to entry then entry would depend on commercial returns from the better value-for-money product being sufficient to overcome the cost of entry. On the other hand, where there is no significant improvement in value-for-money, and low barriers to entry, then entry into this market is as another participant with nothing special to distinguish it from others, whereas if there are high barriers to entry then this business opportunity is harder to access to potential competitors.

The ways that a market disrupting business angle changes the shared search and transaction costs, will then change the structure of the value network. Where the market disruption is from innovation which reduces transaction costs then the value network could expect to promote fragmentation of the value network into more stages. Conversely, increase in transaction costs would be accompanied by vertical integration.

A platform operator who creates a platform that others can access facilitates the development of an ecosystem. This enables other organisations to invest to uncover unanticipated applications products. For the platform operator this reduces the risk of new product development, and increases access to capital to develop products that increase the benefit to users of using the platform. This strategy allows the platform operator to ration its use of its own capital, later acquiring those products developed by others that are revealed to be valuable.

Large scale production processes producing standardise products

A wide range of activity types can be used to construct an MSP+ business angle. Being able to achieve low average unit costs enables platforms to support low prices. Low average unit costs are underpinned by one or more declining cost economies. Sources of declining cost economies are from: economies of scale; improved coordination; scale free networks and the law of large numbers; and information asymmetries. Realising declining cost economies are important to the success of MSP+'s to support low prices. This entails operating large scale standardised processes, with product specifications that support standardised products sold using simple contract types.

Chapter 3
Pricing and the launch of an MSP+

Demand model

As part of the business planning to evaluate the feasibility of a perceived MSP+ business opportunity, high-level models are used. A General Equilibrium model is used in this book to gauge the magnitude of the various elements to the proposed business angle. This type of model does not consider feedback effects, for that Systems Dynamics models are used, but those models can be difficult to calibrate and interpret the results. High-level analysis usually does not have rich data to work with and must rely on guesses, here General Equilibrium models can be useful to understand the key inter-relationships, although giving misleading projections because of the simplifying assumptions that are made because they are unable to take into account feedback loops. The value of General Equilibrium models is not to forecast outcomes, but to tease out relationships that can be used to design market testing experiments, and to be better prepared to be agile in refocusing decisions utilising the new information from market tests. Experience is that desktop models are a tool to formulate hypotheses that when market tested provide valuable, and sometimes surprising insights. This chapter describes a General Equilibrium model for the high-level estimation of the strength of the launch conditions for a new MSP+. It does this by estimating: the size of the area in which positive feedback operates; the prices to the user groups; and market uptake trajectory. It is the model used to generate the graphs described in this book. The value of the variables used are given in the notes to the graphs.

The demand function in Figure 5 in which transactions by senders (S) is related to the strength of senders' desire to reach receivers (E). The full specification of the level of demand on a platform by senders is also influenced by: price (P), general income (Y), taste for the platform product (T), and competing alternatives (A). The relationship is described by the equation below. For simplicity of presentation, the equation is written in its logarithmic form (where the asterisk superscript indicates the log of the variable:

$$S^* = \alpha_S^* + \beta_S P_S^* + \gamma_S Y^* + {}_S E^* + \varepsilon_S T_S^* + \zeta_S A_S^*$$

Equation 1

Where β is the price elasticity of demand, γ the income elasticity of demand, ε the taste elasticity of demand, ζ the elasticity of substitution, and a constant aS > 0 which accounts for the context of the product. A depiction of the relationship in Equation 1 is shown in Figure 5. Similarly, the transaction by receivers for the content (C) from senders is:

$$R^* = \alpha_R^* + \beta_R P_R^* + \gamma_R Y^* + \delta_R C^* + \varepsilon_R T_R^* + \zeta_R A_R^*$$

Equation 2

The reach to achieve the critical mass point is established by substituting the sender demand function into the receiver demand function – this is done by equating reach with the number of receivers (i.e. E = R) and access to content to the number of senders using the platform (i.e. C = S). Where the first derivative of Equation 1 with respect to R is greater (less) than the first derivative of Equation 2 with respect to S then it is the critical mass point.

Simplifying, the critical mass point for receivers is (a corresponding equation can be written for senders):

$$R^* = d\,[\,\tilde{\alpha}^* + \beta_R P_R^* + \delta_R \beta_S P_S^* + (\gamma_R + \delta_R \gamma_S) Y^* + \varepsilon_R T_R^* + \delta_R \varepsilon_S T_S^* + (\xi_R + \delta_R \xi_S) A^*\,]$$

Equation 3

$d=\frac{1}{1-\delta_R \delta_S}$ is the platform cross-group multiplier. One of the important take-outs from Equation 3 is the impact of the cross-group multiplier. The first thing to note is that for values of $\delta_R \delta_S$ less than one, as this product increases, d increases rapidly. As $\delta_R \delta_S$ approaches 1, d becomes very large. In other words, the number of receivers to reach critical mass becomes very small. As $\delta_R \delta_S$ approaches 1, d becomes asymptotic, and for values greater than 1, its sign changes to negative. Then as $\delta_R \delta_S$ becomes large, i.e. there are very strong cross-group effects in operation, the value of d becomes an increasingly small negative value. This means that the other variables make little contribution to determining the critical mass point – this is the condition for a single-sided market. In most instances, the strength of cross-group effects is favourable where $1 \leq \delta <$ say 5, or adverse where $\delta >$ say 10.

The price elasticity of demand is commonly in the range of -0.3 (for an essential item whose consumption changes little in response to a change in price) through to -3.0. – -3.0 means that for a one percent increase in price, sales will fall by 3 percent. The important circumstance to note is where joint cross-group multipliers are large, even small reductions in price to receivers can lead to a significant increase in up take by senders. Price is a variable under the control of management.

Income elasticity of demand y is usually positive, and an economy wide matter outside the control of management but can indicate the contribution to a successful launch a growing economy can have.

Taste for a product, the perceived benefit it gives, is dictated, within its market and society context, by product design, brand and social network effects. Some elements of these factors are under the control of management. Taste elasticity of demand is normally positive, as is seen in the value-for-money (vfm) relationship:

$$vfm^* = \varepsilon T^* - P^*$$

Equation 4

The elasticity of substitution ζ on the other hand is negative for competing substitutes, and positive for complements. As an example, emails and digital channels are strong substitutes of physical mail.

The second important take-out from Equation 3 is the impact of the values of the elasticities of demand. Because some of the elasticities can be negative, the value of the terms in the square brackets can be negative and with $\delta R \, \delta S$ greater than one, the critical mass point increases, and is negative where the value of the terms in the square brackets is positive.

Pricing Framework

Bringing these various pricing relationships together, Figure 10 provides a framework to map the information on a two-sided market. The diagram shows the demand curves for receivers and senders (transposed), and the associated participation curves. For the conditions set out here, critical mass is achieved, and under the right pricing conditions, positive cross-group effects operate to encompass the whole of the addressable market - the point of maximum participation is at the top right-hand corners of the active quadrant. The diagram also shows the price trade-off curve – the trade-off between the higher prices that will constrain usage to the critical mass point, preventing cross-group feedback effects from operating, and the prices achievable at the point of maximum participation (shown as a directional vector).

Figure 10 *Two-sided market pricing framework*

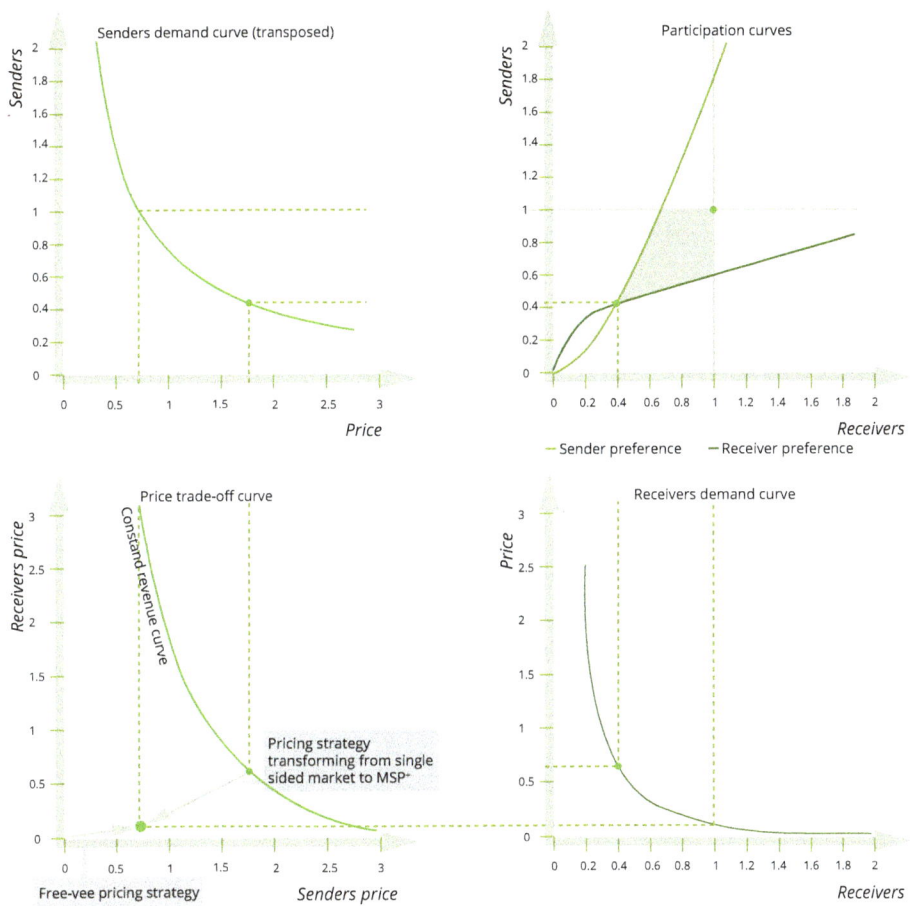

Note to figure: Parameter values are for senders, price elasticity of demand -1, taste elasticity of demand 1 and value of 1, cross-group elasticity of demand of 1.5, and preference elasticity of demand -0.5 and value of 1. For receivers, price elasticity of demand -0.5, taste elasticity of demand 1 and value of 1, cross-group elasticity of demand of 3.0, and preference elasticity of demand -0.5 and value of 1.

Pricing to the user groups

To provide context to the price trade-off to move from the critical mass point to the point of maximum participation, the constant revenue curve at the critical mass point is also shown in the bottom left-hand graph in Figure 10. Platform revenue (ρ) is calculated as:

$$\rho^* = (P_R^* + R^*)*(P_S^* + S^*)$$

Equation 5

Focusing on the price relationship by setting the constant to 1, elasticities for income, taste, and alternatives to 0, Equation 1 reduces to:

$$R^* = \beta_R P_R^* + \delta_R S^*$$

Equation 6

Where R and S are less than or equal to 1. 1 corresponds to the whole addressable market using the platform. Substituting in Equation 5, platform revenue is:

$$\rho^* = ((1 + \beta_R) P_R^* + \delta_R S^*)*(P_S^* + S^*)$$

Equation 7

With the operation of positive cross-group effects, revenue depends on the price to senders and receivers, the receiver price elasticity of demand, and access to content from senders. The revenue equation can also be written from the senders' point of view, which reaches the same conclusions except from the sender's point of view.

Setting prices above the prices to maintain the point of maximum participation will constrain usage. Setting prices above prices at the critical mass point will further constrain usage, and will extinguish positive cross-group feedback effects. One of the implications of this is that a sure way to destroy an MSP⁺ is to price at a high level to one or both user groups to cause the cross-group effects to collapse. Some universal postal operators have done this.

The free vee – an indicator of the pricing challenge

The price trade-off curve points to a second pricing strategy, applicable for new platforms, that is to use price as a means of transitioning from market entry with the aim, from the start, to price to attain the point of maximum participation. However, the size of the launch challenge is shown by the unshaded area in the active quadrant at bottom left of Figure 10. This unshaded area is called the free-vee because, in the absence of a large enough user group in which to launch, price is an important mechanism to attract users onto the platform. The size and shape of the free vee is a measure of the challenge involved in monetising a platform. A wide (narrow) free vee is a significant (insignificant) challenge to overcome. The free-vee becomes significant where one of the user groups has inelastic price elasticity of demand (i.e. $0 > \beta > -1$) because usage is insensitive to a change in price.

For existing products market analysis can establish the point of maximum participation. For an entirely new proposition, a priory it is impossible to assess the offerings perceived value. For this a minimum viable product market launch is required for market testing, supported by customer feedback mechanisms to evaluate and refine the value proposition. To support the planning of the market testing, General Equilibrium models are useful for providing insights into the pricing estimates for the various user groups. To illustrate the use of this analysis, using conditions in Figure 10, for launch 40 percent of receivers and 45.1 percent of senders are required to use the service in order to reach the critical mass point.

Attaining this market share means that positive price can be charged – provided that price keeps the trajectory in the area where the sender preference curve is above that of the receivers (at that price). At this point positive feedback effects begin to occur and given the conditions in this market all senders and receivers would use the platform's products for free.

The price trade-off curve gives the target price of $0.085 to receivers and $0.786 to senders to be sustainable, and in the absence of competition, positive feedback effects propel uptake through the area in which positive feedback operates to the point of maximum participation at these prices.

Transcending a wide free vee – the freemium pricing model

Freemium pricing is used to address platform launch conditions. It involves a product presented in the market with different value-for-money variants where the lowest value-for-money variant is free, and the higher value-for-money variants have progressively higher prices. The freemium pricing model takes into consideration that, higher value-for-money products are preferred, subject to budget constraints; and that demand for a product can increase through learning from use. Even though the lowest value-for-money product is free, it must provide enough perceived net benefit (after considering all the costs faced by a new user) to provide value-for-money no worse than that of competing products (recall, while the price is free, there are other costs the user faces in using the product, so the full price is not zero).

The freemium pricing model does not have universal applicability to MSP[+]s. The pricing model is appropriate for interface products in an MSP[+]. Products in this setting should meet the following conditions:

- There are several variants of a product that differ in their perceived net benefit to the user (Condition 1); and
- the value-for-money must be positive and significantly different between variants (Condition 2); and

- all variants are designed to drive uptake on the platform and ordered such that as perceived net benefit increases so does the value-for-money (Condition 3); and
- the lowest net benefit/ value-for-money variant is free to the user and there is a price for the other variants (Condition 4).

An illustrative suite of variants of a product (called Entry, Mid-tier and Full spec) that conform to these conditions is depicted in Figure 11. Where there are competing products then the value-for-money relationships as depicted in the curves are already observable in the market:

- The entry level product is free, but the cost to the user is the transaction cost and any associated usage costs. At this cost, the perceived benefit must provide value-for-money no worse than that provided by competing products. The aim of this position is to achieve the critical mass point.
- The mid-tier product, of which there can be several, are positioned on or to the right of the low value-for-money indifference curve and on or above the high value-for-money indifference curve. Taking into account the budget constraints of potential buyers and the objective of growing usage of the platform, mid-tier products tend to be relatively low priced. One such position is shown in Figure 11. The aim of this product is to monetise the product while stimulating positive cross-group effects as usage moves from the critical mass point towards the point of maximum participation.
- The full spec product is priced PS or PR, as relevant. The prices to platform users must be such that business value is positive. The aim of this product is to monetise usage at the point of maximum participation.

Figure 11 *Illustrative suite of variants of a product offering increasing perceived net benefits and value-for-money and the impact on increasing sales to senders due to an increase in number of users from the cross-group effect*

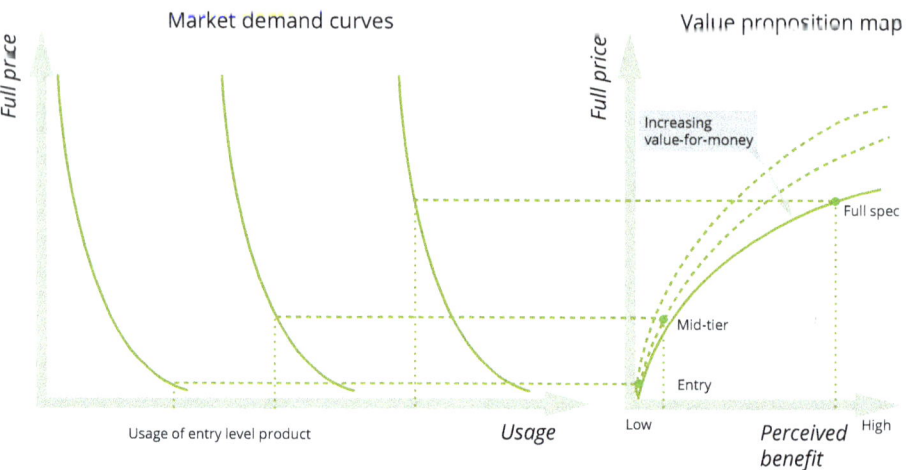

The uptake on a platform is a pricing issue

The implications are these observations to understanding the behaviour of MSP⁺s are:

- Achieving critical mass is a challenge. At least one of the user groups must have a high cross-group elasticity of demand such that δR δS is greater than 1.
- The large values of the joint cross-group multiplier δR δS, the more the management of an MSP⁺ is a pricing issue.
- The initial value of number of senders on the platform can be important. Consequently, having access to an existing user base of potential customers can be an important way to seed an MSP⁺.
- Having achieved critical mass, the platform operator is on a knife edge because as prices are increased, the critical mass point moves further away from the origin. This can make the platform vulnerable to competition and changes in market conditions that change the value of the elasticities.

Chapter 4
Solving the challenges of launch and continued relevance

Market uptake stages

In broad terms, there are three stages in the market uptake of an MSP+. These stages are:

Launch stage characterised by relatively slow growth that is proportional to marketing effort. The aim of launch is to achieve the critical mass point. This stage can involve the commitment of significant resources to marketing.

An explosive growth stage once critical mass is achieved, and positive feedback effects propel take up. The rate of this growth is related to the size of the area in which positive feedback operates (the size of the overlap between the preference curves with senders preference curve above that for receivers). The aim of this stage is to reach the point of maximum participation.

A post turning point stage where the rate of growth slows. The market up take rate slows because the point of maximum participation is being approached, and/or the end of product life cycle is setting in, and/or rivalry from competing offerings reduces market share. The market up take trajectory from this point on depends on which of these reasons is applicable.

An indicator of position in the market up take stages is the rate of customer acquisition for market acquisition effort - for example as measure by the return on marketing investment (ROMI). ROMI is calculated as the incremental margin for the marketing expenditure divided by that additional marketing expenditure. The return on customer acquisition effort at different points in the market uptake stage is:

- Launch, very low, constant return on marketing investment and uptake proportional to effort.
- Explosive growth with very high return on marketing investment driven by positive feedback.
- Post turning point. As the turning point approaches, the return on marketing investment falls until is:
    - Low as the point of maximum participation is reached, and marketing is used to inform users of new functionality which increases the platform's value-for-money to the user groups.
    - Zero as end of product life cycle is reached.
    - Zero due to rivalry from competing offerings, and marketing investment is required to maintain market share.

Improving the chances of a successful launch

The outstanding fact in the creation of valuable MSP⁺s is the need to solve the chicken-and-egg problem of getting enough parties on to a new platform to achieve critical mass. Launch is a severe obstacle for emergent MSP⁺s with most initiatives failing, a challenge exacerbated in small markets. Three key preconditions appear to be important to increase the chances of gaining critical mass:

- having a high value proposition to all user groups; and
- launching into an existing community of users who value the new offering. In this way providing enough early adopters in each user group to be of enough interest to the other group to want to join the platform; and
- focusing on those in the two user groups facing the strongest shared transaction costs.

n this respect, organisations with a large customer base and supporting brand significantly mitigates the launch obstacle. The launch challenge is also reduced by access to other social network effects such as social network and other positive feedback effects, for example those associated with word-of-mouth and product range that can be activated in the push to reach critical mass.

With these preconditions in place, pricing plays a critical role in driving uptake. However, the operation of feedback effects makes it difficult to intuitively assess the net outcome of the business proposition that a valuable business opportunity exits. This is because with strong positive feedback effects pricing on one side of the market can have a disproportionate impact on other user groups – pricing matters.

MSPs can be made more valuable as the strength of positive cross-group feedback increases and the product becomes an essential (i.e. with inelastic price elasticity of demand). This requires continual enhancement of the value propositions to each of the user groups. It can be expected that positive cross-group effects will change with increased usage in the market, for example from learning from use.

The existence of cross-group effects says nothing about the impact of competition – either in terms of the ability to retain customers (disintermediation) or the ability of competitors to coexist in the market.

Positive social network and other behavioural feedback effects can occur in the same markets as cross-group feedback effects. Care needs to be taken in separating the impact of these different effects to manage each's contribution to address the launch challenge.

Market uptake trajectory

Using the scenario depicted in Figure 10 to explore the launch challenge in establishing an MSP[+]. The challenge is tackled from the perspective of estimating the uptake of senders and receivers, and the conditions that need to exist for cross-group effects to operate. Starting with estimates of the participation curves, the implied market development process is to attain the base loads required by each user group. The example shows the first milestone, to reach the critical mass point, is to gain a base load of 45.1 percent of the content (senders), and reach of 40 percent (receivers). These are important milestones. Under the right conditions, crossing the critical mass point then cross-group feedback effects are activated. The second milestone is the point of maximum participation, which in this example is the whole of the addressable market.

Small market size

For any MSP+ market size is an important factor. The market opportunity in a small market requires the participation functions to be enhanced so that the point of critical mass is shifted towards the origin and within the addressable market. Nonetheless, MSP+s can operate at a local level, e.g. fresh produce markets, shopping malls and local newspapers. These examples illustrate that for small market size:

The success of platforms is critically dependant on designing highly valuable propositions for all parties to the platform in the target markets.

The stronger the value proposition and its promotion, the greater the chance that the critical mass point is within the size of the addressable market.

The strength of the positive feedback effects is influenced by the strength of the value propositions to all parties to the platform.

Shopping malls and local newspapers also provide good examples of how cross-group feedback can be lost to competing products, and changes in market conditions.

Competition and disintermediation

A risk faced by MSP+s is for users and competitors to try to bypass the platform. Disintermediation occurs when transacting parties bypass the platform and deal directly with one another. Examples of this are the drive by senders to substitute email for physical mail, and for merchants to substitute electronic banking for credit cards. This threat of disintermediation is one of the strong motivations for platform providers to continually increase the value of the platform to users.

It is also worth noting that the impact of a loss in value to the user can be different for the two preference functions. On its own, a reduction in sender preference because of a reduction in value-for-money, say from a price increase, may be less than the loss in value because of a reduction in the preference to use the platform by receivers for content.

Platforms operating in markets subject to positive feedback are on a knife edge, in that the positive feedback operates to different strengths on the different competing organisations and the strength can change with circumstances. Circumstances, serendipity and the strength of feedback can see a single organisation pull ahead, and others losing market share.

Competitive strategies in MSP+s are:

- Multi-homing. Multi-homing refers to a situation in which competing offers operate alongside one another, with users signing up to competing platforms showing no preference for any of the alternatives. The most well-known example of multi-homing is credit cards. The aim of a multi-homing strategy for platform providers is to split the market for transactions.
- Provide full interoperable compatibility with the dominant player then cherry pick the market. The aim of this strategy is to try to get the dominant player to behave as if they were operating in a single-sided market and competing in a single market and neglecting the other sides of the market, and their feedback effects.
- Maintenance of incompatibility. The aim of this strategy is to segment the market. The reward from this strategy is from the sale of applications products, such as apps, music, video, and games which are not available on the other mobile phone operating systems. This

strategy is an option where the market is large enough to support several competing MSPs.

Competitors who succeed in splitting a market may reduce the market share faced by each organisation below critical mass, eliminating any advantage from positive feedback effects. In the extreme case a market disrupting business angle could undermine the revenue model of an existing MSP⁺. For example, the revenue model of newspapers based on classified adverts has been disrupted by auction sites and search engines.

Maintaining on-going relevance

Because MSP's insert themselves in a value network to facilitate transactions between parties, disintermediation is a threat to platform operators. To guard against this, platforms must ensure they are removing, and continually remove, significant costs from the market which the parties would face when operating outside of the platform. All MSP⁺s face the risk of disintermediation. The demise of the postal network shows how rapidly MSP⁺s can demise, and how vulnerable MSP⁺s are to disintermediation.

Profitability depends on realising declining cost economies

To be profitable, at the maximum participation point the value of the average unit cost must be on or below and to the left of the price trade-off curve. This usually requires the platform provider to realise declining cost economies. Failure to achieve this means the platform has negative business value.

For some platforms, significant losses may need to be sustained to build scalable systems and processes before the level of usage of the platform are such that the pricing on the price trade-off curve is achieved, and the platform made profitable.

Chapter 5
Evaluating the potential of an emergent MSP+

Wide range of business angles

The examples of MSP+s given in Figure 1 illustrate that high search and shared transaction costs are found in a wide range of settings. Identifying a new emergent opportunity focuses on locating in a value network at least two groups transacting with one another who face high search and shared transaction costs. Search costs cover all costs incurred in finding a party including the cost of making a second-best choice because the first best alternative could not be found. Shared or duplicated transaction costs cover all costs incurred from the time of the desire to commence a commercial exchange through to its satisfactory conclusion. Furthermore, identifying a new opportunity requires that these transacting groups are subject to positive cross-group feedback effects. That is, for example, access to greater reach of receivers is appealing to senders, and access to more content from senders is appealing to receivers.

For an existing MSP+, there may be opportunities to broaden the MSP+ by growing the user base, and adding new product offerings. Whether there are new extension opportunities can be ascertained by identifying for each product group the underlying sources of value-for-money to each party, and counter parties they transact with. Expansion opportunities can be in the form of extending existing products to these groups; or by introducing new products that bring new user groups on to the platform.

The value propositions to each group

The benefits a platform provides users are:

- removes significant search and shared transaction costs; and

- does not interfere with the relationship between the transacting parties; and
- improves access to reach for senders and content for receivers; and
- provides better value-for-money compared to the alternatives available.

In addition, these benefits less the full cost to use the platform should exceed the opportunity cost of leaving the platform once a relationship between senders and receivers is established.

Whether the perceived opportunity could disrupt the market can be established by, first, estimating the magnitude of increase in value-for-money, and second, gauging the strength of the barriers to entry. First, the magnitude of the increase in value-for-money. Buyers choose, subject to their budget, the product which provides the best value-for-money. A product disrupts the market where it is widely available by offering value-for-money that is so superior to alternatives that it causes a change in buyer behaviour. The calculation of the potential size of the market disruption requires: identifying the alternatives available, and then for each alternative the sources of benefit, the characteristics of buyers, the number of buyers and the search and shared transaction costs involved. A component of these costs is the contract used - where simple contract types impose least cost. Simple contracts are used where: it is easy to assess supplier performance; the cost of measuring performance is low; the risk adjusted cost of failure is low; and the asset specificity is low.

In offering products with high value-for-money, the platform operator tries to design a product that effectively provides barriers to disintermediation by the transacting parties; and barriers to entry by competitors. Barriers are strengthened by: high capital costs, strong declining cost economies and no capacity constraints; and strong cross-group feedback, and information to tailor the product offering to user requirements.

Potential for positive cross-group feedback effects

The Valhalla conditions that are conducive to launch, e.g. because of low critical mass, are.

- Senders participation curve is above and to the right of the receivers participation curve, and the critical mass point is within the addressable market.
- Price elasticity of demand for each user group is < 0.
- Price is set to attain the point of maximum participation, that maximises the usage by the user groups.

MSP⁺s can begat other MSP⁺s because, being in the business of removing shared transaction cost they come across other opportunities, have the user base and brand reputation to solve the launch challenge, and declining cost economies to provide high value-for-money.

Overcoming the launch challenge

For the platform provider, having identified an opportunity, the challenge to overcome in launching is to reach critical mass. The conditions to realise this are:

- Creating enough value-for-money for each of the multiple user groups transacting over the platform.
- Removing shared transaction costs faced by the user groups.
- Stimulating positive feedback effects between the different user groups such that it increases the attractiveness to other users to use the platform.
- There are enough early adopters in each user group to be of sufficient interest to the counter party group to want to use the platform.

With these conditions satisfied, pricing is used to drive uptake, and for this the freemium pricing model can be useful.

The platform is valuable to the operator

Having identified a potential opportunity, the design challenge is to specify platform products and a production process that does not insert itself in the relationship between the parties, while at the same time providing:

- high benefit through the removal of transaction costs at a price to drive uptake to the point of maximum participation.
- the platform operator with the ability to capture part of the value added.
- to operate the production process profitably. This requires a production process that has strong declining cost economies.

Framework for evaluating the prospects of an emergent MSP⁺

An assessment of a perceived platform opportunity providing significant reductions in shared search and transaction costs without intervening in the relationship between the transacting parties might, on the surface, indicate potential for an MSP. Where, in addition it is assessed that strong positive cross-group effects can be stimulated, then there is potential that this is an MSP⁺. The objective in distilling an MSP⁺ opportunity is to locate a value proposition for a platform in which all these factors strongly contribute.

In summary, the key questions evaluating the potential existence of an MSP⁺ intermediating between two user groups consisting of senders and receivers are:

1. Can a platform product be defined that facilitates transactions between multiple parties without taking part in the transaction (the precondition) such that:

A. comparative value-for-money of senders transacting with receivers is improved; and

    B. comparative value-for-money of receivers transacting with senders is improved?

2. Are search and shared transaction costs between the user groups reduced compared to the alternatives available experienced by:

    C. senders; and

    D. receivers?

3. Can strong cross-group effects be stimulated between the user groups because:

    E. many receivers participating on the platform is beneficial to senders; and

    F. many senders participating on the platform is beneficial to receivers?

4. Are there prospects that the critical mass point is within the addressable market (g)?

5. Is the platform expected to be valuable to the platform operator (h)?

The coat hanger model is a pictorial representation of the transaction, feedback loops and shared transaction and search costs which are encapsulated in an MSP⁺ - it is depicted in Figure 12. The analogy to a coat hanger is to make the point that without each of the user groups gaining substantial benefit compared to alternatives, and strong cross-group effects, then the coat hanger fails to provide support. This support, however, is conditional on solving the launch challenge to achieve critical mass, and being valuable. Because of the impact of feedback effects, to assess whether the perceived opportunity holds any prospect of success a model is required, the framework presented in Figure 10 is one such model.

Figure 12 *Coat hanger model used as an analogy for the conditions for an MSP*[+]

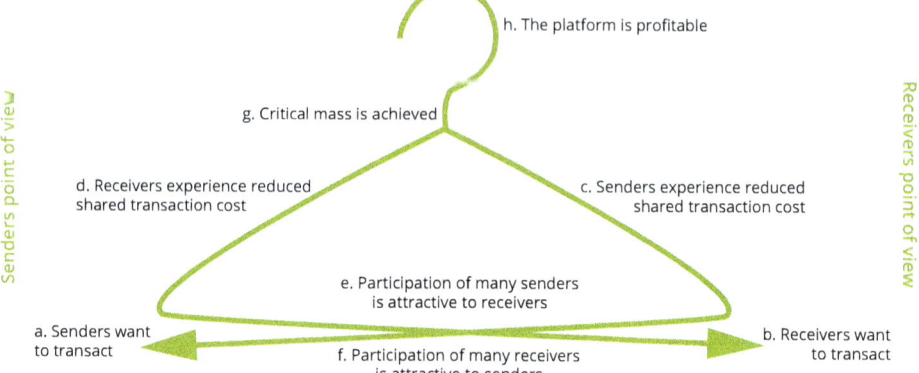

Key influences on the work

Because of the enormous value that some businesses have been able to achieve, Research into MSPs is a rapidly growing field. For an introduction to MSPs see the 2011 working paper by Hagiu and Wright *Multi-Sided Platforms* from Harvard University.

There is a wide literature on General Equilibrium models stretching back to the pivotal work by Lord Marshal in 1890.

The use of participation curves to analyse MSP's is explored by Evans and Schmalensee in the paper *Failure to launch: Critical mass in platform businesses* published in 2010 in the Review of Network Economics.

On transaction costs see for example Oliver Williamson's papers 'Transaction-Cost Economics: The Governance of Contractual Relations' in a 1979 edition of *Journal of Law and Economics*.

The ideas underpinning this book are derived from Hughes, *The Drive of Business: Strategies for Creating Business Angles*, published in 2016.

The examples used in the text draw from consulting projects undertaken by Hughes Consulting Limited.

Abbreviations

C – Content, a product attribute provided by the platform to receivers

E – Reach, a product attribute benefit provided by the platform to senders

FCF – Free cash flow – see profit

MSP – Multisided platform

MSP^+ – Multisided platform with positive cross-group effect

n – Number of players

P – Total price to consume/use

R – Receivers, the counter party user group

T – Taste for a product which is related to its benefit

S – Senders, one of the user groups

vfm – Value -from-money

Y – Income

α – Constant in the demand function within a context

β – Price elasticity of demand

γ – Income elasticity of demand

δ – Cross-group elasticity of demand

ε – Taste elasticity of demand

d – Platform cross-group multiplier

ρ – Platform revenue

Glossary

Activity type – Activity type is the specific method used in the production process to transform acquired inputs into delivered outputs.

Addressable market – The addressable market is the customers that can be reached by the organisation.

Aggregate method – Aggregate method provides products by operate capabilities using the knowhow, systems and processes that depend on the law of large numbers and scale-free infrastructure networks.

Application products – Application products extend the use of knowhow, systems and processes to new adjacent workflow processes or value networks by providing functionality.

Arbitrage method – Arbitrage method applies knowhow, systems, and processes to identify differences in the price of products and resources that are caused by asymmetries in information and high transaction cost. This method relies on transaction specific knowledge, which can arise from barriers to information, location, time, customer relationships, etc.

Assemble method – Assemble method uses knowhow, systems, and processes to produce products by exploiting economies of scale and scope.

Asset – 1. Assets are products with positive value that the organisation has rights of ownership or control.

2. Assets are stocks of benefits and include tangible assets (e.g. land, building, machinery, tools, and inventory) and intangible assets (e.g. goodwill, patents, working capital and bank accounts). Assets may not have a market value and are recorded in the Balance Sheet following GAAP.

Assign method – Assign method produces products using knowhow, systems, and processes to operate capabilities that gain efficiencies by improving coordination, by ensuring close alignment of the interests between principals and agents.

Behavioural feedback effects – Behavioural feedback effects relate to buyer behaviours such as cross product and product group effects, cross-group effects, social network, and reputational effects. The feedback effect can be positive, neutral, or negative.

Benefit – Benefit is derived from product attributes that can be real, service attributes and include intangible benefits from product meaning, brand association, fashion, and bandwagon effects, to name a few.

Boundary of the organisation – Boundary of the organisation refers to the scope of the activities undertaken within an organisation.

Brand – Brand refers to notoriety and reputation. Positive brand can be associated with ease of access to buyers and providers, lower transaction costs, increased transactions, and higher margins. Brand is frequently equated to a person, product, organisation, or idea.

Business – Business is any entity engaged in exploiting a business angle. A business can be a business unit within an existing corporate, a new start-up venture, consortium, joint venture, or a businessperson operating on their own account. A business may or may not be constituted as a legal entity, such as a limited liability company or cooperative society, amongst other forms.

Business angle – A business angle is a perceived opportunity and an activity type to exploit it.

Business model – The business model is the way in which the business opportunity is converted into profit. This covers the activity type including its knowhow, systems and processes, organisational structure, product specifications, and target buyers.

Business opportunity – Business opportunity is an intervention in a market to potentially earn profit.

Business proposition – A business proposition is a description of the business opportunity with the supporting business model to exploit it.

Capability product – The provision of production processes able to perform functions to a specification.

Capacity products – The provision of production processes capable of producing an amount of product to a specification.

Capital – Capital is the funds provided by lenders and investors. The price of capital from lenders is the interest rate charged. The return to investors is a share of profits such as dividends.

Competing alternatives – Buyers have the choice between competing alternatives that include direct competitors offering similar products to the same market, indirect competitors offering a similar product but to a different market segment, and substitute products to the same market.

Contractual commitments – Contractual commitments is a catchall category for items that arise from express terms and conditions between the parties to an agreement, sometimes in the form of a legally binding agreement and which are not otherwise classified as commodities and assets. Contractual commitments are intertwined with the organisation's dealings in all element markets. Importantly contractual claims can create assets as well as liabilities for the organisations. These contracts can be bilateral or trilateral. GAAP and tax authorities have specific rules for the treatment of some contractual commitments.

Coordination mechanism – Products are exchanged according to the coordination mechanisms used between the parties. There are four types of coordination mechanism. Push/push coordination involves the supplier producing products as a precursor to offering them for sale in the market. Push/pull coordination is the production for inventory, that is subsequently drawn down by buyers, or where capacity or capability are put in place to be called on when required. Pull/pull relates to customised production when a product is produced to meet a custom order. Pull/push production is contract production for a buyer's inventory, from which the buyer then draws down their requirements.

Cost of friction – Also called transaction cost.

Critical mass point – The intersections of the receivers and senders participation curves is the critical mass point.

Cross-group effect – Cross group effect is the phenomenon in which demand by one group is influenced by demand by another group. This effect is positive, neutral, or negative.

Cross-product effect – Cross product effect occurs where demand for a product is determined by demand for another product. Examples include substitutes and complements. In some cases, this increase in demand can have a positive feedback effect and increase demand for the original product. For example, size of product range (content) increases so the demand for all products increases (such as devices on which to play the content).

Declining cost economies – Declining cost economies are positive feedback effects that create value added through lower average costs, increasing barriers to entry or lower transaction costs, and include those derived from size, scale and scope achieved in the operation of knowhow, systems, and processes; agency costs, the law of large numbers, scale-free infrastructure networks and density economies; asymmetries in access to information, knowledge, institutional arrangements, and location and time.

Demand curve – A demand curve shows the relationship between price and the quantity of a product bought.

Elasticity of demand – Elasticity of demand is a measure of the proportionate change in quantity demanded as a result of a proportionate change in an independent variable. Important independent variables in the analysis of the responsiveness of demand are price, income and competing products.

Exchange products – Exchange products provide a high degree of readiness for use, through for example, custom, standardisation and specification, and transfer decision-making rights to consume or use to the buyer on sale, if not entirely, then at least for a period.

FCF – Free cash flow – see profit.

FCF value – FCF value is calculated as the net present value of expected future free cash flows.

Feedback effects – Feedback effects refer to the nature of the interrelationship between the attainment of one state (e.g. volume produced) and value of another state (e.g. cost structure). Feedback effects can be supply and demand-side effects and the impact can be positive, negative, or neutral. For example, with the production of more output the impact of positive feedback is declining average costs and negative feedback would result in increasing average costs.

Free-vee – The free-vee is the gap between the origin and the critical mass point as indicated by the participation curves for a two sided market. It indicates the size of the launch challenge to establish an MSP^+.

Friction – Another term for transaction cost.

Information – Information covers data, details, facts, and knowledge about a situation.

Information asymmetries – Information asymmetries refer to situations where one party has better information than others and this causes the parties to behave differently. Information asymmetries arise from constraints on access to data, deficiencies in knowledge, from institutional arrangements, from geographic location, and because of time.

Inputs – In the setting of the definition of profit, an input is any cash expenditure such as on commodities and assets.

Institutional arrangements – Institutional arrangements cover, for instance, social conventions, the law, and agreements.

Interface products – Interface products are associated with the interaction with systems and processes, or channel for delivering exchange products.

Investment – The commitment of assets, including capital, resources, labour (such as in sweat equity) and reputation to an organisation.

Law of large numbers – The phenomenon where, with more occurrences of an unconnected event, the occurrence of an event lies more closely to the average occurrence of the event.

Market – A market is the institutions, social conventions, infrastructure, and capabilities that facilitate the repeated exchange of products, assets, skills, capital, information, and other resources.

Market disruption – A market disruption is a buyer experience that occurs when comparative value-for-money changes rapidly enough to be noteworthy, forcing a re-evaluation of spending patterns.

Method – Method is a set of capabilities with supporting information enabling the acquisition of inputs or delivery of outputs.

MSP⁺ – Multisided platform with positive cross group effects.

Multi-sided platform (MSP) – A multisided platform enables two or more parties to transact directly with one another. This is done by providing the platform for interchanges between various parties, but not actually taking part in the contractual relationship between the parties.

Opportunity cost – The opportunity cost is the net benefit forgone by pursuing the best alternative course of action.

Organisation – Organisation refers to any entity engaged in economic activity to exploit a business angle. In this setting, an organisation can be a business unit within an existing corporate, a new start-up venture, consortium, joint venture, or a businessperson operating on their own account. An organisation may or may not be constituted as a legal entity, such as a limited liability company or cooperative society, charity, amongst other forms.

Organisational ability – Organisational ability refers to knowhow and the operation of organisation wide systems and processes.

Organisational structure – The organisational structure refers to knowledge acquisition, business strategy, organisational architecture, and incentive schemes.

Outputs – In the setting of the definition of profit, an output is any cash income, most importantly products. Some outputs are inputs that are resold.

Participants – Participants are involved with an organisation and in a value network, including buyers, providers, suppliers, competitors, and government.

Participation curve – The participation curve shows the operation of cross group effects, particularly how usage of a platform by one group of users changes with different levels of access to another group of users.

Parties – Parties are the participants in a transaction that involve contractual claims, such as buyers and their suppliers, and principals and agents. For example, there are parties to a contract and participants in a market.

Perceived benefit – The benefits to the buyer including aspirational benefits in the form of its product meaning, such as its allure within the culture and context in which the product is offered for sale.

Platform – A platform is a highly scalable production process that removes a set of shared transaction costs faced by large groups of users.

Point of maximum participation – The point of maximum participation is the maximum share of the addressable market of users that are attracted to use an MSP[+].

Preference curve – The value-for-money relationship between price and perceived benefit is depicted by the preference curve.

Price trade-off curve – The price trade-off curve shows the trade-off between the higher prices that will constrain usage to the critical mass point, preventing cross-group feedback effects from operating, and the prices achievable at the point of maximum participation. It is shown as a directional vector.

Pricing types – A categorisation of different types of pricing based on the market positioning strategy they are to support. 12 types of pricing are discussed: ethical, auction, cost-based, target, relationship-based, attribute, value-based, differential, economic effect, multi-part, negotiated, and dynamic pricing

Product – Product is used as a generic term for items that are exchanged between parties in product markets and have attributes that provide benefits such as service quality.

Product form – Products take the form of access to a capacity to have some function performed, a capability to perform some function, or a complete product.

Product meaning – Product meaning refers to how buyers relate to a product because of connotations associated with its physical, functional, symbolic, and cultural attributes.

Product specification – The product specification describes the product form, type of interconnection with the production processes, and coordination mechanism, as set out in the technical, functional and performance attributes, the amounts, and the terms and conditions of the contract.

Production process – The production process is the overarching term for the collection of capabilities and supporting information used by the organisation. A production process has organisational structure, activity type that uses production technology with appropriate knowhow, systems and processes, resources, and contractual obligations to transform a volume of inputs into outputs.

Product-range effect – The increase in perceived benefit to a buyer in dealing with a supplier because the large range of different products available from the supplier, or the wide range of competing alternatives within a product group are available from the supplier.

Profit – Profit during a period is the net operating profit after tax, less the change in working capital and expenditure required to maintain the operating profit. This definition of profit is also known as free cash flow. An approximation of free cash flow from the financial accounts of a business is EBIT (1 – tax rate) plus depreciation and amortization less change in working capital less expenditure to maintain the current operating capability.

Reputational effects – A behavioural feedback effect associated with notoriety encapsulated in brand and simulacra.

Resource – A resource is a source or supply of profit. To illustrate this concept, whereas real estate property is an asset, the flow of benefits it provides (e.g. shelter, prestige) is a resource. The asset can be sold. By letting real estate the resource is sold. Other examples of resources are labour effort and knowhow.

Return on marketing investment (ROMI) – Return on marketing investment is calculated as the incremental margin for marketing expenditure divided by marketing expenditure.

Risk – 1. The variation from the target value that is anticipated, and its consequences assessed. Risk is management's expectation of the variation, but is only one component of uncertainty. Before the event it is impossible to know the degree to which risk is aligned to the uncertainty.

2. Synonym for uncertainty, connoting exposure to loss which, for example, could result in loss of capital invested.

Scale-free infrastructure networks – Scale-free infrastructure networks relates to production processes, especially infrastructure networks, which involve high initial fixed cost and diminishing unit costs, and which follow a power law relationship for the addition of more users.

Single-sided market – Used for normal markets, that is those that are not multisided markets.

Social network effect – Contagions that occur between people in a group (which can be buyers, sellers, finance providers, friends). These contagions can be spread by word-of-mouth and the bandwagon effect.

Speculation – Speculation is the act of picking a future price for a product or asset.

Stage – Value networks are broken in stages by markets. A stage comprises capabilities organised into one or more nodes.

Strategy – A set of directed actions to realise an objective.

Structural changes – Changes to nature and characteristics of the value network together with the wider institutional, commercial, and social structures in which an organisation operates.

System – 1. A network of capabilities and information flows with resultant behaviour responses to external stimuli. In this meaning an organisation is a system, as is a value network.

2. The equipment, software, plant, machinery, infrastructure, and procedures used in processes following prescribed procedures, which provide the capability and capacity to deliver an organisation's outputs, for example a computer system.

Transaction costs – The costs incurred in the process of organisations transacting are transaction cost. These include searching, negotiating, changes to be able to use the product, ambiguity in scope of the product being contracted for, monitoring performance, invoicing and payment, maintaining documentation and performance failure.

Uncertainty – Uncertainty is the variation from the target value. Uncertainty ranges from risk (that is, the known unknowns in which the likelihood of events occurring can be assessed); through to acknowledgement of unknown knowns, for example, severe rare events where the potential for occurrence is recognised even though their occurrence may be unknown; and on through to unknowable events. These events can occur in all contributors to business value and cover uncertainty in price, opportunity, input, capability, decision, business value, and regulatory and institutional arrangements.

Value – That is business value of FCF value - see FCF value.

Value added – Value added is the difference between the benefit enjoyed by buyers from a product less the cost to produce it. Value added is the sum of the value-for-money to buyers plus the profit to suppliers.

Value controller – An organisation with high bargaining power that exerts a high degree of control over the allocation of value added in a value network can dictate, at least for a period, the pace of change in the value network.

Value network – Value network is a network of capabilities and supporting information, usually from more than one organisation, which culminates in the capacity to deliver products to the final consumer.

Value network map – A value network map is a depiction of the stages in a value network, the participants at each stage as measured by their market share, and the relationship between the participants.

Value proposition – Value proposition is the promise that a product will deliver perceived benefits to the buyer for the price.

Value-for-money – Value-for-money is the difference between the perceived benefit to the buyer of a product and its price.

Value-for-money indifference curve – The value-for-money indifference curve describes the relationship between price and the perceived benefit of the product.

Venture – A business with the connotation of a high speculative component for expected profit.